All rights reserved. No part of this publication may be reproduced, distributed, or transmitted in any form or by any means, including photocopying, recording, or other electronic or mechanical methods, without the prior written permission of the publisher, except in the case of brief quotations embodied in critical reviews and certain other noncommercial uses permitted by copyright law.

For permission requests, write to the publisher:
Laprea Education, Inc.
info@StructuredLiteracy.com

www.StructuredLiteracy.com

ISBN: 979-8-88741-905-3

© 2024 Laprea Education, Inc.

This workbook is intended for use by one SINGLE person. The reproduction of any part of this book for more than one person or for an entire school or school system is strictly prohibited. No part of this publication may be transmitted or recorded in any form without written permission from the publisher.

Table of Contents

Teaching High-Frequency Words	2
Phonemes and Graphemes for the 109 HFW	4
Sentences for High-Frequency Words	5
The 109 High-Frequency Words (in frequency order)	10

the	10	what	41	more	72	after	103
of	11	all	42	her	73	words	104
and	12	were	43	two	74	called	105
a	13	when	44	like	75	just	106
to	14	we	45	him	76	where	107
in	15	there	46	see	77	most	108
is	16	can	47	time	78	know	109
you	17	an	48	could	78	get	110
that	18	your	49	no	80	through	111
it	19	which	50	make	81	back	112
he	20	their	51	than	82	much	113
for	21	said	52	first	83	before	114
was	22	if	53	been	84	go	115
on	23	do	54	its	85	good	116
are	24	will	55	who	86	new	117
as	25	each	56	now	87	write	118
with	26	about	57	people	88		
his	27	how	58	my	89		
they	28	up	59	made	90		
at	29	out	60	over	91		
be	30	them	61	did	92		
this	31	then	62	down	93		
from	32	she	63	only	94		
I	33	many	64	way	95		
have	34	some	65	find	96		
or	35	so	66	use	97		
by	36	these	67	may	98		
one	37	would	68	water	99		
had	38	other	69	long	100		
not	39	into	70	little	101		
but	40	has	71	very	102		

Teaching High-Frequency Words (HFW)

What Are High-Frequency Words?
High-Frequency Words (HFW) are the words that make up the majority of spoken and written words in a language. Once a person can read these words fluently, their reading fluency takes off. There are numerous lists of HFW published in books and online. Some include variations of words that are found on other lists, but it seems that no two lists are exactly the same. This can make it hard to know where to focus efforts when learning HFW.

This book includes the most critical 109 HFW for readers to learn. Equipped with the ability to read these 109 words (and their derivatives) and some basic phonics knowledge, children will be able to read "90 percent of the single syllable words they encounter in texts" (Solity & Vousden, 2009, as cited in Burkins & Yates, 2021). These 109 words are adapted from Adams (1990) and Carroll, Davies, and Richmond (1971) (as cited in Burkins & Yates, 2021) and can also be found among Fry's first 300 words on his Instant Words lists (Burkins & Yates, 2021).

How Should We Teach High-Frequency Words?
Many HFW have irregular parts. Irregular parts are those that cannot be decoded, or read, by students using basic phonics knowledge. For example, the word "said" has the irregular part "ai" that is read with the short "e" sound rather than the long "a" sound seen in words like "pail" and "faint." This can tempt some to teach these words through memorization; however, that is not what we want to do if we want students to add the word to their long-term mental bank of words. Instead, we want to teach the words and point out the irregular parts.

<u>When first introducing</u> a HFW, we recommend using the "Read, Spell, Write, Extend" technique (Blevins, 2024). The technique is as follows:
1. Start with the sentences. Write a sentence that contains the word where the learner can see it. Underline the high-frequency word. Read the sentence aloud, pointing to the high-frequency word as you read it. Have the learner repeat the word.
2. Have the learner write the high-frequency word. Ask them to underline the parts of the word they know and draw a heart around the parts they do not know. For example, consider the word "want." They might know that the "w" represents the /w/ sound, the "n" represents the /n/ sound, and the "t" represents the /t/ sound, but they may not realize that the "a" doesn't represent the normal short a /ă/ sound. So you would underline the "w," "a," and "t" while drawing a heart around the "a" to show that it is irregular.

<u>Once the HFW has been introduced</u>, have the learner practice with the word using the worksheets in this book. First, they trace the letters then use the remaining space on the lines to write the word. Next, they color in the letters of the word, giving them more familiarity with each letter. Then, the learner practices distinguishing the word from similar words by circling it each time they find it in a group of words. After that, the learner cuts apart the letter tiles and glues them in order to properly spell the word. Finally, the learner reads each occurrence of the word on the page by dragging a finger under the letters while saying the sounds out loud.

<u>To review previously taught HFW</u>, display the completed worksheets of the 20 most recently taught HFW on a wall or bulletin board and ask the learner to read through them several times a day. Each time a new word is added, replace the oldest word with it so that learners are only reviewing the previously taught 20 words. For most learners, these 20 additional days of exposure will help them master each word. If there are words that your learner struggles with, however, feel free to leave the specific words up for a longer period of time and cycle through words they have mastered instead.

In What Order Should I Teach the High-Frequency Words?
The words are currently listed in the book in order of frequency in the English language. Some people choose to introduce them in frequency order, 2-5 words per week. Another suggestion is to introduce them according to similarities. You can use the lists below to introduce groups of words together at the same time. The common characteristic is noted in the heading of each list. ("Simple" signifies words that follow common spellings, and "tricky" signifies one or more parts that might be temporarily or permanently irregular. *Temporarily irregular* means that students have not yet learned the phonics rule to sound out part(s) of the word. *Permanently irregular* means the word has a part that is considered irregular in the English language, no matter how much phonics knowledge the learner has. Limit introduction of "tricky" words to 1-3 at a time.)

References
Blevins, W. (2024). *Differentiating phonics instruction for maximum impact: How to scaffold whole-group instruction so all students can access grade-level content.* Corwin Literacy. *Corwin*.

Burkins, J., & Yates, K. (2021). *Shifting the balance: 6 ways to bring the Science of Reading into the Balanced Literacy classroom.* Stenhouse Publishers. 480 Congress Street, Portland, ME 04101.

Closed Syllable Words: Often the first words learners can decode are closed syllable words. These words represent the short vowel sounds and basic consonant sounds.
- With Two Letters (simple): **in, it, on, at, an, if, up**
- With Two Letters (tricky): **is, as, of**
- With Three Letters (simple): **had, not, but, can, him, did, get**
- With Three Letters (tricky): **was, his, has**
- With Blends (simple): **and, just**
- With Blends (tricky): **from, find, most**

Words with Digraphs: Digraphs are letter combinations that represent a single sound. Some of the most common digraphs are ff /f/, ll /l/, ss /s/, zz /z/, ck /k/, sh /sh/, ch /ch/, th /th/ or /th/, wh /w/ or /hw/, ng /ng/.
- Words (simple): **will, that, with, this, when, which, them, then, than, back, much, long**
- Words (tricky): **all, the, what**

Words with Magic E: These words include a silent "e" at the end of the word that actually has an important job; it signifies that the preceding vowel represents its long sound.
- Words (simple): **like, time, make, made, use**
- Words (tricky): **have, one, were, there, some, these, where, write**

Words with Vowel Teams: Regular vowel teams are vowel combinations that represent a single vowel sound. Some of the most common vowel teams are ai /ā/, ay /ā/, ee /ē/, ea /ē/, ey /ē/, oa /ō/, oe /ō/, ow /ō/, ie /ī/, igh /ī/, ew /ū/ or /yū/, ue /ū/, ui /ū/, and the most common diphthongs are oy /oy/, oi /oy/, ow /ow/, ou /ow/.
- Words (simple vowel teams): **each, see, way, may**
- Words (simple diphthongs): **about, how, out, now, down**
- Words (tricky): **they, their, said, would, two, could, been, people, know, through, you, good**

Words with R-Controlled Vowels: Often the letter "r" affects how the vowel preceding it is pronounced; sometimes it alters its sounds, and other times it makes it nearly impossible to hear a vowel sound at all. Common r-controlled vowels are ar /ar/, or /or/, ore /or/, er /er/, ir /er/, ur /er/.
- Words (simple): **for, or, more, her, first, after, words**
- Words (tricky): **are, your, other, water, very**

Words with Open Syllables: When a vowel is the last letter in a syllable, it often represents its long sound.
- Words (simple): **a, he, be, I, we, she, so, no, over, before, go**
- Words (tricky): **to, do, into, who**

Other Words
These words represent syllables that end with "y" (single syllable words represent the /ī/ sound, and two-syllable words represent the /ē/ sound).
- Words (simple): **by, my**
- Words (tricky): **many, only**

This word represents a word with a stable final syllable "le": **little**.
This word represents the base word "call" with the suffix "ed": **called**.

Phonemes and Graphemes for the 109 HFW

The 109 high-frequency words are listed below, along with their phonemes, or sounds (P) and graphemes (G), which are the spellings that make the sounds. Use the graphemes for word mapping exercises. The underlined parts signify that the part is irregular and doesn't follow normal phonics rules.

Word	P	G	Word	P	G	Word	P	G	Word	P	G
the	th/ə	th/e	what	hw/ə/t	wh/a/t	more	m/or	m/ore	after	ă/f/t/er	a/f/t/er
of	ə/v	o/f	all	aw/l	a/ll	her	h/er	h/er	words	w/or/d/z	w/or/d/s
and	ă/n/d	a/n/d	were	w/er	w/ere	two	t/ū	t/wo	called	k/aw/l/d	c/a/ll/ed
a	ə	a	when	hw/ĕ/n	wh/e/n	like	l/ī/k	l/i/ke	just	j/ŭ/s/t	j/u/s/t
to	t/ū	t/o	we	w/ē	w/e	him	h/ĭ/m	h/i/m	where	hw/ā/r	wh/e/re
in	ĭ/n	i/n	there	th/ā/r	th/e/re	see	s/ē	s/ee	most	m/ō/s/t	m/o/s/t
is	ĭ/z	i/s	can	k/ă/n	c/a/n	time	t/ī/m	t/i/m/e	know	n/ō	kn/ow
you	y/ū	y/ou	an	ă/n	a/n	could	k/oo/d	c/oul/d	get	g/ĕ/t	g/e/t
that	th/ă/t	th/a/t	your	y/or	y/our	no	n/ō	n/o	through	th/r/ū	th/r/ough
it	ĭ/t	i/t	which	hw/ĭ/ch	wh/i/ch	make	m/ā/k	m/a/ke	back	b/ă/k	b/a/ck
he	h/ē	h/e	their	th/ā/r	th/ei/r	than	th/ă/n	th/a/n	much	m/ŭ/ch	m/u/ch
for	f/or	f/or	said	s/ĕ/d	s/ai/d	first	f/ir/s/t	f/ir/s/t	before	b/ē/f/or	b/e/f/ore
was	w/ə/z	w/a/s	if	ĭ/f	i/f	been	b/ĭ/n	b/ee/n	go	g/ō	g/o
on	ŏ/n	o/n	do	d/ū	d/o	its	ĭ/t/s	i/t/s	good	g/oo/d	g/oo/d
are	ar	are	will	w/ĭ/l	w/i/ll	who	h/ū	wh/o	new	n/ū	n/ew
as	ă/z	a/s	each	ē/ch	ea/ch	now	n/ow	n/ow	write	r/ī/t	wr/i/te
with	w/ĭ/th	w/i/th	about	ə/b/ow/t	a/b/ou/t	people	p/ē/p/l	p/eo/p/le			
his	h/ĭ/z	h/i/s	how	h/ow	h/ow	my	m/ī	m/y			
they	th/ā	th/ey	up	ŭ/p	u/p	made	m/ā/d	m/a/de			
at	ă/t	a/t	out	ow/t	ou/t	over	ō/v/er	o/v/er			
be	b/ē	b/e	them	th/ĕ/m	th/e/m	did	d/ĭ/d	d/i/d			
this	th/ĭ/s	th/i/s	then	th/ĕ/n	th/e/n	down	d/ow/n	d/ow/n			
from	f/r/ə/m	f/r/o/m	she	sh/ē	sh/e	only	ō/n/l/ē	o/n/l/y			
I	ī	I	many	m/ĕ/n/ē	m/a/n/y	way	w/ā	w/ay			
have	h/ă/v	h/a/ve	some	s/ŭ/m	s/o/m	find	f/ī/n/d	f/i/n/d			
or	or	or	so	s/ō	s/o	use	yū/z	u/se			
by	b/ī	b/y	these	th/ē/z	th/e/se	may	m/ā	m/ay			
one	w-ə/n	o/n	would	w/oo/d	w/oul/d	water	w/aw/t/er	w/a/t/er			
had	h/ă/d	h/a/d	other	ə/th/er	o/th/er	long	l/ŏ/ŋ	l/o/ng			
not	n/ŏ/t	n/o/t	into	ĭ/n/t/ū	i/n/t/o	little	l/ĭ/t/l	l/i/tt/le			
but	b/ŭ/t	b/u/t	has	h/ă/z	h/a/s	very	v/ă/r/ē	v/e/r/y			

Sentences for the HFW

the	1. The cat ran faster than the dog. 2. Can you hand me the bag of chips? 3. I see the big brown fish in the water.	**on**	1. I put my backpack on the counter. 2. Did you write your name on the paper? 3. The fat cat sat on the mat.
of	1. Can I have a piece of cake? 2. Did you get a big slice of pizza? 3. How many of the peaches did you get?	**are**	1. Are you going to eat those hot fries? 2. We are going to ride bikes to the park. 3. My favorite colors are pink and teal.
and	1. I have a big dog and a little cat. 2. Do you want chicken nuggets and fries? 3. He put on his socks and shoes.	**as**	1. The cow is as big as a car. 2. I am not as tall as my mom! 3. I wish I was as fast as a lion!
a	1. A big bee buzzed by the yellow flower. 2. Can I get a chocolate milk, please? 3. There is a beautiful rainbow in the sky!	**with**	1. I go with my mom to the grocery store. 2. I like to eat french fries with ketchup. 3. I wear socks with my shoes.
to	1. I will go to my grandma's house today. 2. We had to take my dog to the vet. 3. She is going to the zoo.	**his**	1. The boy made his bed. 2. The man wanted to wash his car. 3. My brother put away all of his laundry.
in	1. Please put your bag in the car. 2. Did you put the dishes in the box? 3. My teacher told me to turn in my paper.	**they**	1. They sat while they talked on the bench. 2. My friends said they are coming over. 3. They went on a walk through the forest.
is	1. This is the best kind of apple! 2. What is your favorite color? 3. Is this your backpack on the floor?	**at**	1. We are finally at the beach! 2. I went to sit at the table with my dad. 3. My mom and dad are at work.
you	1. You are a very smart and funny kid! 2. Will you please help me with this job? 3. Can you come to my birthday party?	**be**	1. We need to be on the bus at noon. 2. This will be an easy book to read. 3. I want to be a teacher when I grow up.
that	1. Can I have that banana? 2. That is the dog's bed! 3. We need to take that back to the store.	**this**	1. This is the last day of the month. 2. Is this blue jacket yours? 3. May I have some of this pie?
it	1. I like that shirt because it is cute! 2. Take the toy and put it in the box. 3. Choose a cookie and eat it.	**from**	1. This present is from my aunt and uncle. 2. I got this flower from the yard. 3. My brother took my ball from me.
he	1. My brother runs fast when he plays tag. 2. My dad says he loves me! 3. He put the toolbox in the shed.	**I**	1. My mom and I eat cereal for breakfast. 2. I hope I get a red bike for my birthday. 3. My friends and I like to play tag.
for	1. Will you please get the laundry for me? 2. This big gift is all for me! 3. I will draw a picture for my mom.	**have**	1. I have to go to the dentist today. 2. Do you have to go to the bathroom? 3. Do you have a pencil I can borrow?
was	1. The cow was mooing very loudly. 2. Was the trip to the zoo fun today? 3. My hamburger was so good!	**or**	1. Do you want mint or cookie ice cream? 2. Is your bike blue or green? 3. Would you like to get a pet fish or bird?

by	1. I parked my car by the tree. 2. Will you please sit by me at lunch? 3. My dog likes to sleep by me at night.	**which**	1. Which crayon do you like best? 2. Do you know which chips you would like? 3. Which pair of shoes are yours?
one	1. I put one sandwich in my lunchbox. 2. Can I please use one of your crayons? 3. You may play for one more minute.	**their**	1. The kids put their toys in the toy box. 2. My family likes to make their own pizzas. 3. Dogs like to run or walk with their people.
had	1. My mom said I had to clean my room. 2. I had eggs for breakfast this morning. 3. My dad had to get up early for work.	**said**	1. My mom said I had to go to bed. 2. "Let's go to the zoo," said Dad. 3. Who said we had to come in right now?
not	1. I am sick, so I am not going to school. 2. My pet cat is not very old. 3. It is not sunny outside.	**if**	1. My friend asked if I could come over. 2. I can go if I get my room cleaned. 3. If the pie is too hot, you should let it cool.
but	1. I like bananas, but I do not like apples. 2. He likes math, but reading is his favorite. 3. She wants to go, but she is too tired.	**do**	1. Do you want to go out to dinner tonight? 2. He has a lot of work to do today! 3. I do not want to do my homework.
what	1. What is your favorite type of cracker? 2. Do you know what that sound was? 3. What time is it right now?	**will**	1. Will you go to the movies with me? 2. My dad will go to the store for my mom. 3. After school I will go to swim class.
all	1. All of my friends go to my school! 2. The boy ate all of his dinner. 3. All the crayons fell onto the floor.	**each**	1. We each got a new pair of shoes. 2. I got one of each color. 3. Each of us got a colorful popsicle.
were	1. We were going to the zoo, and it rained. 2. Were you happy with your steak? 3. Why were you hiding from me?	**about**	1. I am about done with my dessert. 2. He is about to lose a tooth. 3. What is this book about?
when	1. When do I have to go to bed? 2. My mom calls me when dinner is ready. 3. I get up when it is time to go to school.	**how**	1. How did you get your work done so fast? 2. Can you tell me how to do this problem? 3. How many hot dogs can you eat?
we	1. We went to a basketball game last night. 2. We are wearing the same purple shirt! 3. Where are we going for dinner?	**up**	1. The fox was up a tree. 2. He climbed up the ladder. 3. The vase is up on the top shelf.
there	1. I see a small turtle over there. 2. Did you see the huge plant over there? 3. There will be no school today!	**out**	1. I need to take the dog out for a walk. 2. The ball bounced out of bounds. 3. We walked out the door.
can	1. I will ask my dad if I can go to the park. 2. Can I get a grape soda from the fridge? 3. The girl can do a cartwheel!	**them**	1. My mom said I could play with them. 2. The kids asked me to sit next to them. 3. He lost his socks, and he cannot find them.
an	1. An elephant played in the water. 2. Can you put an apple in my lunchbox? 3. I found an earring on the ground.	**then**	1. He ran fast, then he got some water. 2. First we go to the store, then we cook. 3. I danced and then I took a nap.
your	1. What is your name? 2. Is that your bike parked next to mine? 3. I like your new shoes!	**she**	1. She looks so cute in that outfit! 2. My sister asked me if she could play. 3. Mom is hungry, and she wants a snack.

many	1. How <u>many</u> markers are in the box? 2. Do you have <u>many</u> quarters in your bank? 3. I do not have <u>many</u> socks to choose from.	**time**	1. What <u>time</u> does the movie start? 2. My mom said it is <u>time</u> to go to bed. 3. Is it <u>time</u> to go to the game?
some	1. <u>Some</u> of my friends go to my gym. 2. I asked my dad if I could have <u>some</u> money. 3. Do you have glue, or do you need <u>some</u>?	**could**	1. <u>Could</u> you please get the toys for me? 2. The girl <u>could</u> not ride her bike. 3. The cat <u>could</u> run very fast.
so	1. I missed the bus, <u>so</u> I had to walk. 2. He hung up the painting <u>so</u> it could dry. 3. We like our teacher <u>so</u> much!	**no**	1. "Oh, <u>no</u>!" yelled the girl. 2. I had <u>no</u> idea this pie would be so good. 3. <u>No</u>, you may not get a snack right now.
these	1. <u>These</u> are the prettiest flowers! 2. Where did you get <u>these</u> delicious cookies? 3. Whose pens are <u>these</u>?	**make**	1. What did you <u>make</u> in art class today? 2. "Will you <u>make</u> cookies?" I asked Mom. 3. Please <u>make</u> a card to go with your gift.
would	1. <u>Would</u> you like to go to the play with me? 2. I <u>would</u> really like to go to the movies. 3. Where <u>would</u> I find the best tacos?	**than**	1. The elephant is bigger <u>than</u> the hippo. 2. I would rather go swimming <u>than</u> running. 3. My pink shirt is smaller <u>than</u> my blue shirt.
other	1. I went to the store the <u>other</u> day. 2. Do you want this one or the <u>other</u> one? 3. Please hand me the <u>other</u> book.	**first**	1. The boy is going into <u>first</u> grade. 2. <u>First</u>, you need to get a sheet of paper. 3. Who will be the <u>first</u> to clean up?
into	1. Did you put the chicken <u>into</u> the oven? 2. The boy put his shoes <u>into</u> the shoebox. 3. The bus driver got <u>into</u> the bus.	**been**	1. It has <u>been</u> too long since I have seen you! 2. I have not <u>been</u> on a vacation in years. 3. Max has <u>been</u> such a good cat.
has	1. The dog <u>has</u> a treat in her bowl. 2. <u>Has</u> the timer gone off yet? 3. My dad <u>has</u> to go to work tomorrow.	**its**	1. I put the pencil in <u>its</u> case. 2. The snail hid down deep in <u>its</u> shell. 3. The fish swam into <u>its</u> hole.
more	1. Can I have some <u>more</u> spaghetti? 2. Do you want <u>more</u> snacks in your bag? 3. I have six <u>more</u> addition problems to do.	**who**	1. <u>Who</u> stole the cookie from the cookie jar? 2. Do you know <u>who</u> won the game? 3. <u>Who</u> sells the corn at the farmers market?
her	1. <u>Her</u> pet bunny is very soft. 2. I really like <u>her</u> little red wagon. 3. The girl and <u>her</u> mom go to the park.	**now**	1. <u>Now</u> is the time to dance in the rain. 2. Do I have to go to bed right <u>now</u>? 3. I am <u>now</u> taller than my brother.
two	1. Is it <u>two</u> o'clock already? 2. The squirrel has <u>two</u> nuts in her nest. 3. The baby claps his <u>two</u> hands together.	**people**	1. How many <u>people</u> can fit in the elevator? 2. The <u>people</u> waited in the long line. 3. Did you see all the <u>people</u> at the concert?
like	1. Do you <u>like</u> to have milk with your cookies? 2. I <u>like</u> to draw rainbows with markers! 3. The hamster does not <u>like</u> to roll in the ball.	**my**	1. <u>My</u> mom is the best mom! 2. <u>My</u> dog loves to run around the yard. 3. "This is <u>my</u> book," I said.
him	1. The boy took his backpack with <u>him</u>. 2. My dad took me to the game with <u>him</u>. 3. My dog wants me to chase <u>him</u>.	**made**	1. My dad <u>made</u> hamburgers for dinner. 2. I <u>made</u> a picture for my grandpa. 3. Have you <u>made</u> the cupcakes yet?
see	1. The dog can <u>see</u> the bee flying around her. 2. Did you <u>see</u> the dolphin swimming by us? 3. I <u>see</u> better with my glasses.	**over**	1. The cow did not jump <u>over</u> the moon. 2. Can you please put the book <u>over</u> there? 3. When the game is <u>over</u>, we drive home.

did	1. <u>Did</u> you get a new pair of shoes? 2. The clown <u>did</u> a funny trick. 3. I <u>did</u> all of my math facts!	**just**	1. Can I have <u>just</u> one more piece of candy? 2. My birthday is <u>just</u> days away. 3. I will clean my room in <u>just</u> a minute.
down	1. The mole went <u>down</u> into his hole. 2. I fell <u>down</u> at recess. 3. She put her tray <u>down</u> on the table.	**where**	1. <u>Where</u> should I put my lunch box? 2. <u>Where</u> did you get that cute shirt? 3. <u>Where</u> is Max the cat?
only	1. Are you an <u>only</u> child? 2. I am the <u>only</u> one wearing red today. 3. He will <u>only</u> have one slice of bread.	**most**	1. I am in school <u>most</u> of the day. 2. Peaches are my <u>most</u> favorite fruit. 3. <u>Most</u> of my shirts are a shade of blue.
way	1. Which <u>way</u> do you think we should go? 2. This is the <u>way</u> you use your scissors. 3. Which <u>way</u> did the fox go?	**know**	1. I <u>know</u> all the sounds in the alphabet! 2. Do you <u>know</u> where the bathroom is? 3. I do not <u>know</u> all my math facts.
find	1. Will you <u>find</u> me if we play Hide-and-Seek? 2. Do you think the dog will <u>find</u> her bone? 3. Where did you <u>find</u> that beautiful sweater?	**get**	1. I will <u>get</u> my lunch and take it to the table. 2. What did you <u>get</u> for your birthday? 3. Can we <u>get</u> new books from the library?
use	1. "Did you <u>use</u> my glue stick?" he asked. 2. I will <u>use</u> my scissors to cut the paper. 3. She will <u>use</u> her ten frame during math.	**through**	1. She looked <u>through</u> the window. 2. The puppy went <u>through</u> the door. 3. My mom looked <u>through</u> her purse.
may	1. <u>May</u> I please use your pencil? 2. I <u>may</u> or <u>may</u> not be able to go. 3. It <u>may</u> depend on the rain.	**back**	1. I put the book <u>back</u> on the shelf. 2. My mom and I walked <u>back</u> home. 3. I lost my bag, so I went <u>back</u> to look for it.
water	1. The frog hopped in the <u>water</u>. 2. Do you like to drink milk or <u>water</u>? 3. My mom put <u>water</u> into the bathtub.	**much**	1. How <u>much</u> does the new car cost? 2. I love you very, very <u>much</u>! 3. The soccer ball cost way too <u>much</u>.
long	1. How <u>long</u> will I have to wait in line? 2. The <u>long</u> snake slithered along the road. 3. Is the box <u>long</u> or short?	**before**	1. <u>Before</u> I go to bed, I brush my teeth. 2. I have to clean my room <u>before</u> I can go. 3. Will we eat <u>before</u> or after the game?
little	1. The <u>little</u> dog barked all the way home. 2. I can't ride the bike because I'm too <u>little</u>. 3. Can I have a <u>little</u> bit of your yogurt?	**go**	1. The man will <u>go</u> to the gym. 2. My mom said I can <u>go</u> to the party. 3. That car can <u>go</u> really fast!
very	1. The <u>very</u> tiny bug crawled on my arm.. 2. I want a <u>very</u> small piece of cake. 3. He was <u>very</u> happy to be picked for the team.	**good**	1. My mom says I have very <u>good</u> manners. 2. Dinner tonight was so <u>good</u>! 3. Eating fruit is <u>good</u> for you.
after	1. <u>After</u> the game, we went out for dinner. 2. What do I do <u>after</u> I read the book? 3. Recess comes <u>after</u> lunch.	**new**	1. I got a <u>new</u> outfit to wear to the show. 2. My dad bought me a <u>new</u> ball. 3. The girl got five <u>new</u> heart words this week.
words	1. How many <u>words</u> are in this sentence? 2. I know many heart <u>words</u>! 3. Chapter books have a lot of <u>words</u> in them.	**write**	1. I will <u>write</u> a letter to my grandpa. 2. The girl knows how to <u>write</u> all her letters. 3. Please <u>write</u> your name on the line.
called	1. My mom <u>called</u> my grandma on the phone. 2. I <u>called</u> for my dog to come to me. 3. The coach <u>called</u> out a play to the player.		

This page is intentionally blank.

the

Name

Write-It

the

Color-It

the

Find-It

| the | these | the | that |
| this | with | the | from |

Build-It

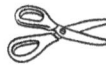

When cutting out the boxes on the left, do not cut this area. The letters for the next word are printed on the other side of this page.

h   t   e

Learning High-Frequency Words © Laprea Education

of

Name

Write-It: of _____

Color-It: of

Find-It:

| from | of | at | of |
| our | on | of | for |

Build-It:

f   o

When cutting out the boxes on the left, do not cut this area. The letters for the next word are printed on the other side of this page.

and

Name

Write-It: and

Color-It: and

Find-It:

| are | and | at | and |
| can | car | and | all |

Build-It:

n a d

When cutting out the boxes on the left, do not cut this area. The letters for the next word are printed on the other side of this page.

12

Learning High-Frequency Words © Laprea Education

Name

Write-It

a

Color-It

a

Find-It

a　　an　　I　　a

all　　be　　a　　can

Build-It

When cutting out the boxes on the left, do not cut this area. The letters for the next word are printed on the other side of this page.

to

Name

Write-It

to

Color-It

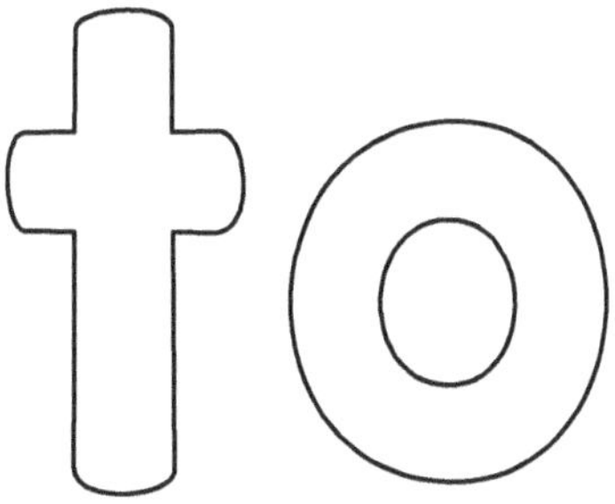

t o

Find-It

| two | to | the | they |
| to | at | stop | to |

Build-It

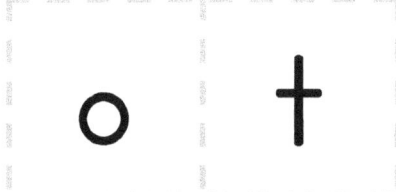

o   t

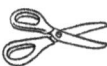

When cutting out the boxes on the left, do not cut this area. The letters for the next word are printed on the other side of this page.

14   Learning High-Frequency Words © Laprea Education

in

Name

Write-It: in

Color-It: in

Find-It:

with   in   on   an

and   an   in   in

Build-It:

When cutting out the boxes on the left, do not cut this area. The letters for the next word are printed on the other side of this page.

is

Name

Write-It

is

Color-It

is

Find-It

| on | is | is | an |
| an | if | his | is |

Build-It

s   i

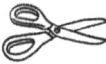

When cutting out the boxes on the left, do not cut this area. The letters for the next word are printed on the other side of this page.

you

Name

Write-It

you

Color-It

you

Find-It

| your | you | use | you |
| up | are | you | all |

Build-It

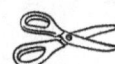

When cutting out the boxes on the left, do not cut this area. The letters for the next word are printed on the other side of this page.

u　y　o

that

Name

Write-It

that

Color-It

that

Find-It

| the | that | this | back |
| that | what | that | then |

Build-It

h   t   t   a

When cutting out the boxes on the left, do not cut this area. The letters for the next word are printed on the other side of this page.

18

Learning High-Frequency Words © Laprea Education

it

Name

Write-It

Color-It

it

Find-It

| an | it | this | an |
| in | it | is | it |

Build-It

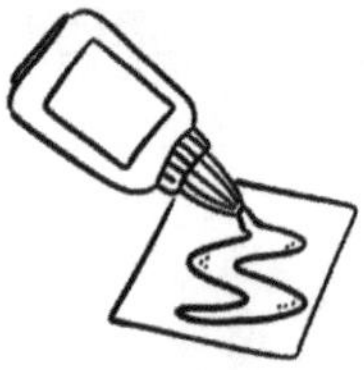

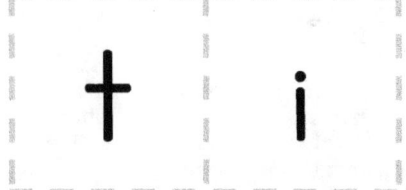

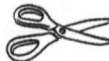

When cutting out the boxes on the left, do not cut this area. The letters for the next word are printed on the other side of this page.

he

Name

Write-It: he

Color-It: he

Find-It:
has   had   he   he
be   he   how   his

Build-It:

e   h

When cutting out the boxes on the left, do not cut this area. The letters for the next word are printed on the other side of this page.

for

Name

Write-It
for

Color-It
for

Find-It

| find | do | of | for |
| for | for | from | or |

Build-It

r f o

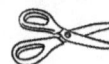

When cutting out the boxes on the left, do not cut this area. The letters for the next word are printed on the other side of this page.

was

Name

Write-It

was

Color-It

was

Find-It

| as | with | was | has |
| was | was | who | way |

Build-It

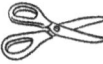

When cutting out the boxes on the left, do not cut this area. The letters for the next word are printed on the other side of this page.

s a w

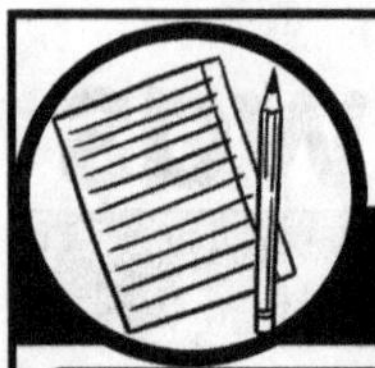

on

Name

Write-It

on

Color-It

on

Find-It

| on | an | at | on |
| no | on | or | for |

Build-It

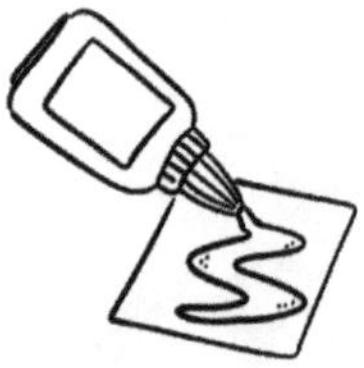

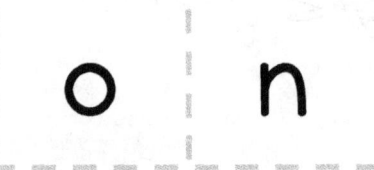

When cutting out the boxes on the left, do not cut this area. The letters for the next word are printed on the other side of this page.

are

Name

Write-It

are

Color-It

are

Find-It

| are | and | at | are |
| can | car | are | all |

Build-It

e　a　r

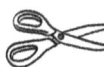

When cutting out the boxes on the left, do not cut this area. The letters for the next word are printed on the other side of this page.

as

Name

Write-It

as

Color-It

as

Find-It

| as | and | at | as |
| all | an | as | by |

Build-It

| s | a |

When cutting out the boxes on the left, do not cut this area. The letters for the next word are printed on the other side of this page.

25

Learning High-Frequency Words © Laprea Education

with

Name

Write-It

with

Color-It

with

Find-It

| will | with | write | it |
| with | the | who | with |

Build-It

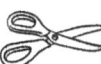

When cutting out the boxes on the left, do not cut this area. The letters for the next word are printed on the other side of this page.

| i | t | w | h |

his

Name

Write-It: his

Color-It: his

Find-It:

| his | his | how | its |
| is | has | her | his |

Build-It:

i s h

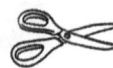

When cutting out the boxes on the left, do not cut this area. The letters for the next word are printed on the other side of this page.

Learning High-Frequency Words © Laprea Education

they

Name

Write-It

they

Color-It

they

Find-It

| with | this | they | they |
| time | they | these | the |

Build-It

h   y   t   e

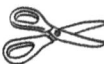

When cutting out the boxes on the left, do not cut this area. The letters for the next word are printed on the other side of this page.

28

at

Name

Write-It	at -------------------
Color-It	at
Find-It	as and at all at an a at
Build-It	

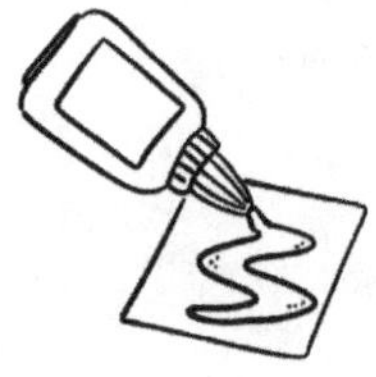

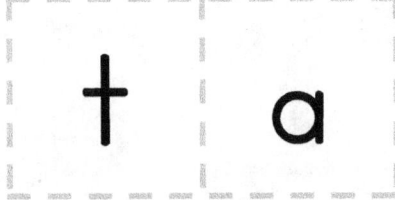

When cutting out the boxes on the left, do not cut this area. The letters for the next word are printed on the other side of this page.

be

Name: _____

Write-It: be ---------------------------

Color-It: be

Find-It:

| been | but | be | be |
| before | be | by | he |

Build-It:

When cutting out the boxes on the left, do not cut this area. The letters for the next word are printed on the other side of this page.

e | b

this

Name

Write-It: this

Color-It: this

Find-It:

| his | this | they | is |
| this | them | two | this |

Build-It:

i t s h

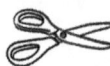

When cutting out the boxes on the left, do not cut this area. The letters for the next word are printed on the other side of this page.

Learning High-Frequency Words © Laprea Education

from

Name

Write-It: from

Color-It: from

Find-It:

find	or	from	first
from	from	for	find

Build-It:

r m f o

When cutting out the boxes on the left, do not cut this area. The letters for the next word are printed on the other side of this page.

Learning High-Frequency Words © Laprea Education

Name

Write-It

I

Color-It

I

Find-It

| I | if | I | a |
| is | I | in | into |

Build-It

I

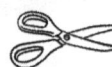

When cutting out the boxes on the left, do not cut this area. The letters for the next word are printed on the other side of this page.

Learning High-Frequency Words © Laprea Education

have

Name

Write-It

have

Color-It

have

Find-It

| has | had | him | have |
| how | have | have | her |

Build-It

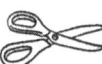

| a | v | h | e |

When cutting out the boxes on the left, do not cut this area. The letters for the next word are printed on the other side of this page.

Learning High-Frequency Words © Laprea Education

or

Name

Write-It

or

Color-It

or

Find-It

| do | or | of | or |
| if | or | on | for |

Build-It

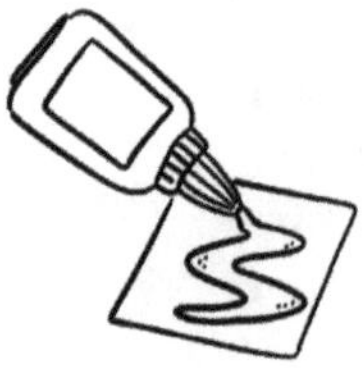

When cutting out the boxes on the left, do not cut this area. The letters for the next word are printed on the other side of this page.

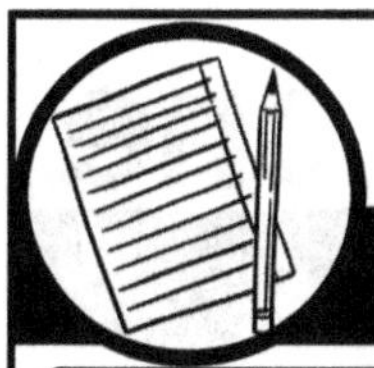

by

Name

Write-It

by

Color-It

by

Find-It

by	my	be	by
buy	an	by	but

Build-It

y b

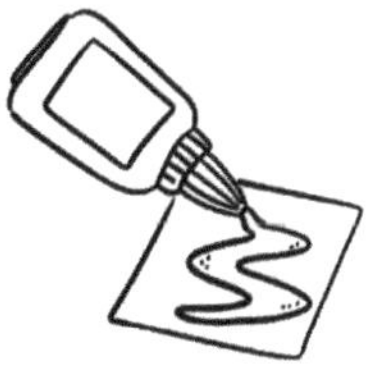

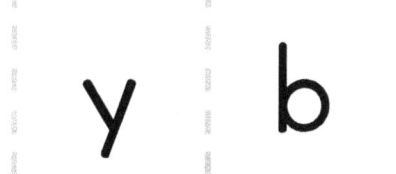

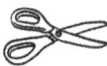

When cutting out the boxes on the left, do not cut this area. The letters for the next word are printed on the other side of this page.

one

Name

Write-It

one

Color-It

one

Find-It

| only | one | or | one |
| no | one | of | not |

Build-It

e o n

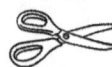

When cutting out the boxes on the left, do not cut this area. The letters for the next word are printed on the other side of this page.

had

Name

Write-It

had

Color-It

had

Find-It

| had | and | had | his |
| has | had | have | how |

Build-It

d h a

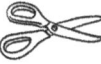

When cutting out the boxes on the left, do not cut this area. The letters for the next word are printed on the other side of this page.

Learning High-Frequency Words © Laprea Education

not

Name _____

Write-It	not _____
Color-It	**not**
Find-It	no not to out now new not not
Build-It	

o   t   n

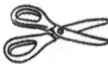

When cutting out the boxes on the left, do not cut this area. The letters for the next word are printed on the other side of this page.

but

Name

Write-It

but

Color-It

but

Find-It

| but | been | by | at |
| by | be | but | but |

Build-It

u b t

When cutting out the boxes on the left, do not cut this area. The letters for the next word are printed on the other side of this page.

what

Name

Write-It

what

Color-It

what

Find-It

that	water	was	what
what	way	what	when

Build-It

t	h	w	a

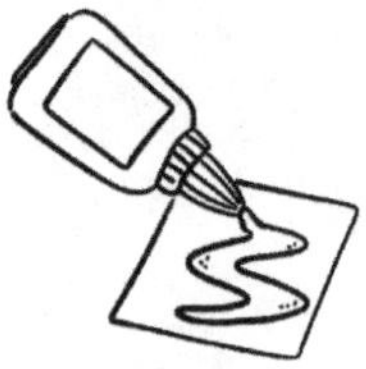

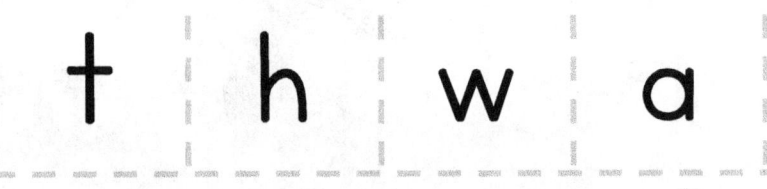

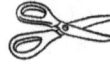

When cutting out the boxes on the left, do not cut this area. The letters for the next word are printed on the other side of this page.

all

Name

Write-It

all

Color-It

all

Find-It

| after | and | all | at |
| all | are | can | all |

Build-It

| l | a | l |

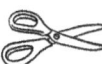

When cutting out the boxes on the left, do not cut this area. The letters for the next word are printed on the other side of this page.

were

Name

Write-It

were

Color-It

were

Find-It

| with | will | were | were |
| were | where | when | what |

Build-It

e e w r

When cutting out the boxes on the left, do not cut this area. The letters for the next word are printed on the other side of this page.

43

Learning High-Frequency Words © Laprea Education

when

Name

Write-It: when

Color-It: when

Find-It:

| then | when | when | them |
| were | will | write | when |

Build-It:

e n w h

When cutting out the boxes on the left, do not cut this area. The letters for the next word are printed on the other side of this page.

Learning High-Frequency Words © Laprea Education

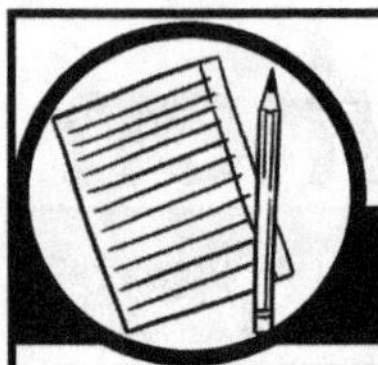

we

Name

Write-It

we

Color-It

we

Find-It

we	be	we	will
were	he	where	we

Build-It

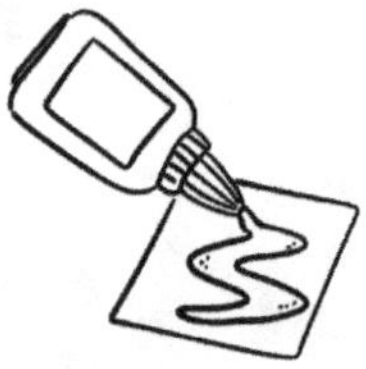

e w

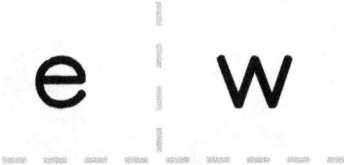

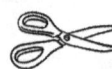

When cutting out the boxes on the left, do not cut this area. The letters for the next word are printed on the other side of this page.

there

Name

Write-It

there

Color-It

there

Find-It

| here | there | are | there |
| there | them | this | they |

Build-It

When cutting out the boxes on the left, do not cut this area. The letters for the next word are printed on the other side of this page.

r e t h e

Learning High-Frequency Words © Laprea Education

can

Name

Write-It	can
Color-It	can
Find-It	can and an at could did can can
Build-It	

n a c

When cutting out the boxes on the left, do not cut this area. The letters for the next word are printed on the other side of this page.

47

Learning High-Frequency Words © Laprea Education

an

Name

Write-It

an

Color-It

an

Find-It

| an | and | at | an |
| all | an | can | for |

Build-It

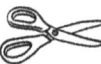

When cutting out the boxes on the left, do not cut this area. The letters for the next word are printed on the other side of this page.

n a

your

Name

Write-It
your

Color-It
your

Find-It

| you | use | out | your |
| your | our | your | over |

Build-It

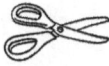

When cutting out the boxes on the left, do not cut this area. The letters for the next word are printed on the other side of this page.

r o y u

which

Name

Write-It: which

Color-It: which

Find-It:

| which | when | we | way |
| what | where | which | which |

Build-It:

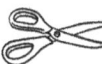

When cutting out the boxes on the left, do not cut this area. The letters for the next word are printed on the other side of this page.

50

Learning High-Frequency Words © Laprea Education

their

Name

Write-It
their

Color-It
their

Find-It

the   they   their   their

these   their   this   to

Build-It

r e t h i

When cutting out the boxes on the left, do not cut this area. The letters for the next word are printed on the other side of this page.

51

Learning High-Frequency Words © Laprea Education

said

Name

Write-It

said

Color-It

said

Find-It

| said | she | did | said |
| see | said | so | some |

Build-It

When cutting out the boxes on the left, do not cut this area. The letters for the next word are printed on the other side of this page.

| a | i | s | d |

if

Name

Write-It

if ----

Color-It

if

Find-It

is   for   if   of

as   if   if   first

Build-It

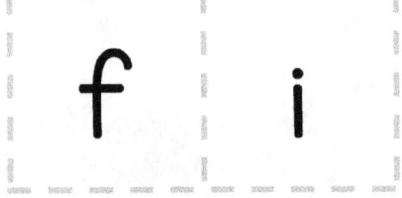

f   i

When cutting out the boxes on the left, do not cut this area. The letters for the next word are printed on the other side of this page.

do

Name

Write-It

do

Color-It

do

Find-It

| does | down | had | do |
| do | of | do | go |

Build-It

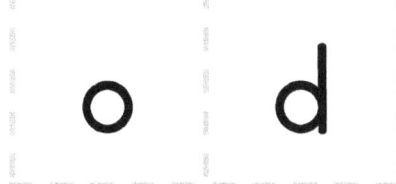

o   d

When cutting out the boxes on the left, do not cut this area. The letters for the next word are printed on the other side of this page.

will

Name

Write-It

will

Color-It

will

Find-It

| will | we | will | write |
| which | was | with | will |

Build-It

When cutting out the boxes on the left, do not cut this area. The letters for the next word are printed on the other side of this page.

| i | l | w | l |

55

Learning High-Frequency Words © Laprea Education

each

Name

Write-It

each

Color-It

each

Find-It

| each | be | each | which |
| much | each | are | an |

Build-It

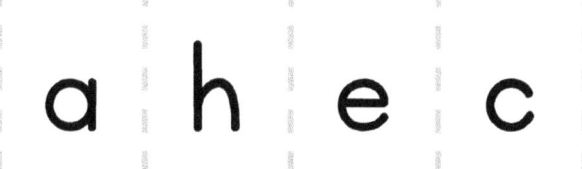

When cutting out the boxes on the left, do not cut this area. The letters for the next word are printed on the other side of this page.

56 Learning High-Frequency Words © Laprea Education

about

Name

Write-It

about

Color-It

about

Find-It

| have | about | always | and |
| about | above | about | give |

Build-It

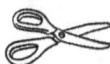

u a t b o

When cutting out the boxes on the left, do not cut this area. The letters for the next word are printed on the other side of this page.

how

Name

Write-It

how

Color-It

how

Find-It

| how | him | her | have |
| he | has | how | how |

Build-It

o w h

When cutting out the boxes on the left, do not cut this area. The letters for the next word are printed on the other side of this page.

Learning High-Frequency Words © Laprea Education

up

Name

Write-It

up

Color-It

up

Find-It

| up | use | just | up |
| but | an | up | out |

Build-It

When cutting out the boxes on the left, do not cut this area. The letters for the next word are printed on the other side of this page.

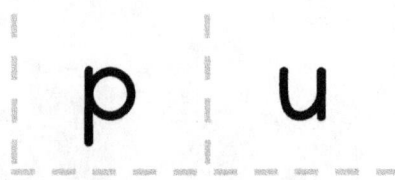

Learning High-Frequency Words © Laprea Education

out

Name

Write-It
out

Color-It
out

Find-It

| out | one | only | out |
| or | other | out | over |

Build-It

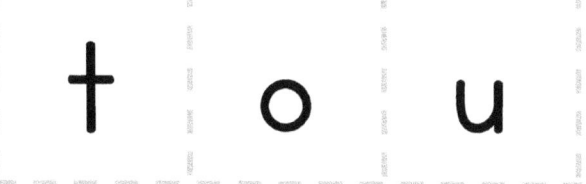

t o u

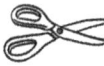

When cutting out the boxes on the left, do not cut this area. The letters for the next word are printed on the other side of this page.

them

Name

Write-It: them

Color-It: them

Find-It:

| them | their | this | that |
| the | them | than | them |

Build-It:

When cutting out the boxes on the left, do not cut this area. The letters for the next word are printed on the other side of this page.

h   m   t   e

then

Name

Write-It
then

Color-It
then

Find-It

| then | them | than | then |
| the | their | then | they |

Build-It

n   h   t   e

When cutting out the boxes on the left, do not cut this area. The letters for the next word are printed on the other side of this page.

62

Learning High-Frequency Words © Laprea Education

she

Name

Write-It: she

Color-It: she

Find-It:

| she | so | she | he |
| said | this | she | was |

Build-It:

h e s

When cutting out the boxes on the left, do not cut this area. The letters for the next word are printed on the other side of this page.

Learning High-Frequency Words © Laprea Education

many

Name

Write-It: many

Color-It: many

Find-It:

| many | made | may | more |
| most | and | many | many |

Build-It:

a n m y

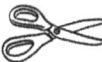

When cutting out the boxes on the left, do not cut this area. The letters for the next word are printed on the other side of this page.

Learning High-Frequency Words © Laprea Education

some

Name

Write-It: some

Color-It: some

Find-It:

some	so	she	some
see	some	one	no

Build-It:

m e s o

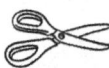

When cutting out the boxes on the left, do not cut this area. The letters for the next word are printed on the other side of this page.

so

Name

Write-It

so

Color-It

so

Find-It

| some | she | so | so |
| so | see | of | go |

Build-It

When cutting out the boxes on the left, do not cut this area. The letters for the next word are printed on the other side of this page.

o   s

 **these**

Name

Write-It: these

Color-It:

Find-It:

| the | them | he | these |
| these | these | see | than |

Build-It:

e e t h s

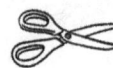
When cutting out the boxes on the left, do not cut this area. The letters for the next word are printed on the other side of this page.

67

Learning High-Frequency Words © Laprea Education

would

Name

Write-It: would

Color-It: would

Find-It:

| would | could | were | would |
| when | out | would | words |

Build-It:

u l d w o

When cutting out the boxes on the left, do not cut this area. The letters for the next word are printed on the other side of this page.

other

Name _____

Write-It

other _____

Color-It

other

Find-It

| out | her | only | other |
| other | over | other | them |

Build-It

r o t e h

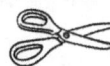

When cutting out the boxes on the left, do not cut this area. The letters for the next word are printed on the other side of this page.

69

Learning High-Frequency Words © Laprea Education

into

Name

Write-It

into

Color-It

into

Find-It

| in | to | into | its |
| into | into | two | it |

Build-It

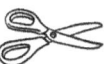

When cutting out the boxes on the left, do not cut this area. The letters for the next word are printed on the other side of this page.

t i o n

70

Learning High-Frequency Words © Laprea Education

has

Name

Write-It: has

Color-It: has

Find-It:

| has | his | had | has |
| how | has | him | as |

Build-It:

s a h

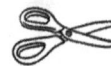

When cutting out the boxes on the left, do not cut this area. The letters for the next word are printed on the other side of this page.

Learning High-Frequency Words © Laprea Education

more

Name

Write-It

more

Color-It

more

Find-It

most   more   make   more

more   made   or   many

Build-It

e   o   m   r

When cutting out the boxes on the left, do not cut this area. The letters for the next word are printed on the other side of this page.

72

Learning High-Frequency Words © Laprea Education

her

Name

Write-It: her

Color-It: her

Find-It:
has her him his
how are her her

Build-It:

e r h

When cutting out the boxes on the left, do not cut this area. The letters for the next word are printed on the other side of this page.

73

Learning High-Frequency Words © Laprea Education

two

Name

Write-It: two

Color-It: two

Find-It:

| time | two | to | two |
| time | two | through | the |

Build-It:

o　t　w

When cutting out the boxes on the left, do not cut this area. The letters for the next word are printed on the other side of this page.

74

Learning High-Frequency Words © Laprea Education

like

Name

Write-It: like

Color-It: like

Find-It:

| like | little | long | it |
| into | its | like | like |

Build-It:

i e k l

When cutting out the boxes on the left, do not cut this area. The letters for the next word are printed on the other side of this page.

him

Name

Write-It: him

Color-It: him

Find-It:

| him | he | her | his |
| how | from | him | him |

Build-It:

When cutting out the boxes on the left, do not cut this area. The letters for the next word are printed on the other side of this page.

see

Name

Write-It

see

Color-It

see

Find-It

| see | said | see | she |
| some | are | see | these |

Build-It

e | s | e

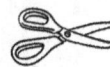

When cutting out the boxes on the left, do not cut this area. The letters for the next word are printed on the other side of this page.

Learning High-Frequency Words © Laprea Education

time

Name

Write-It: time

Color-It: time

Find-It:

| its | this | time | time |
| they | time | two | him |

Build-It:

e m t i

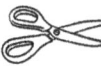

When cutting out the boxes on the left, do not cut this area. The letters for the next word are printed on the other side of this page.

could

Name

Write-It: could

Color-It: could

Find-It:

could   called   always   could
about   could   can   would

Build-It:

d u c l o

When cutting out the boxes on the left, do not cut this area. The letters for the next word are printed on the other side of this page.

no

Name

Write-It

no

Color-It

no

Find-It

no	not	at	no
of	no	know	for

Build-It

o n

When cutting out the boxes on the left, do not cut this area. The letters for the next word are printed on the other side of this page.

make

Name

Write-It

make

Color-It

make

Find-It

| make | made | many | make |
| may | make | more | my |

Build-It

a m k e

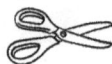

When cutting out the boxes on the left, do not cut this area. The letters for the next word are printed on the other side of this page.

than

Name

Write-It
than

Color-It
than

Find-It

there   than   than   time

them   then   they   than

Build-It

a h t n

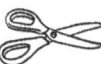

When cutting out the boxes on the left, do not cut this area. The letters for the next word are printed on the other side of this page.

Learning High-Frequency Words © Laprea Education

first

Name

Write-It: first

Color-It: first

Find-It:

| first | from | for | first |
| is | his | first | give |

Build-It:

s r f i t

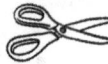

When cutting out the boxes on the left, do not cut this area. The letters for the next word are printed on the other side of this page.

been

Name

Write-It: been

Color-It: been

Find-It:

| been | ball | been | back |
| be | at | been | but |

Build-It:

n b e e

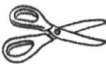

When cutting out the boxes on the left, do not cut this area. The letters for the next word are printed on the other side of this page.

its

Name

Write-It

its

Color-It

its

Find-It

| its | it | if | its |
| his | its | in | into |

Build-It

When cutting out the boxes on the left, do not cut this area. The letters for the next word are printed on the other side of this page.

85

Learning High-Frequency Words © Laprea Education

who

Name

Write-It

who

Color-It

who

Find-It

| who | we | how | who |
| was | words | who | you |

Build-It

h o w

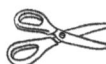

When cutting out the boxes on the left, do not cut this area. The letters for the next word are printed on the other side of this page.

now

Name

Write-It: now

Color-It: now

Find-It:
| now | no | know | now |
| not | most | now | one |

Build-It:

---

w n o

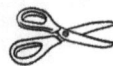

When cutting out the boxes on the left, do not cut this area. The letters for the next word are printed on the other side of this page.

people

Name

Write-It: people

Color-It: people

Find-It:

| people | about | always | through |
| about | people | people | give |

Build-It:

e p l e o p

When cutting out the boxes on the left, do not cut this area. The letters for the next word are printed on the other side of this page.

my

Name

Write-It

my

Color-It

my

Find-It

my much may my

make my many made

Build-It

When cutting out the boxes on the left, do not cut this area. The letters for the next word are printed on the other side of this page.

made

Name

Write-It

made

Color-It

made

Find-It

| made | make | made | many |
| may | most | much | made |

Build-It

a d m e

When cutting out the boxes on the left, do not cut this area. The letters for the next word are printed on the other side of this page.

over

Name

Write-It

over

Color-It

over

Find-It

| over | only | one | over |
| other | of | over | out |

Build-It

v r o e

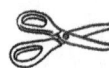

When cutting out the boxes on the left, do not cut this area. The letters for the next word are printed on the other side of this page.

did

Name

Write-It: did

Color-It: did

Find-It:

| did | do | down | did |
| could | said | did | good |

Build-It:

i d d

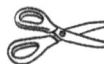

When cutting out the boxes on the left, do not cut this area. The letters for the next word are printed on the other side of this page.

Learning High-Frequency Words © Laprea Education

down

Name

Write-It
down

Color-It
down

Find-It

| down | do | down | did |
| how | at | an | down |

Build-It

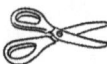
When cutting out the boxes on the left, do not cut this area. The letters for the next word are printed on the other side of this page.

w d n o

only

Name

Write-It

only

Color-It

only

Find-It

| only | one | on | only |
| over | out | only | most |

Build-It

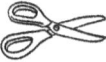

y　n　l　o

When cutting out the boxes on the left, do not cut this area. The letters for the next word are printed on the other side of this page.

94

Learning High-Frequency Words © Laprea Education

way

Name

Write-It: way

Color-It: way

Find-It:

| way | was | as | way |
| who | you | way | what |

Build-It:

y w a

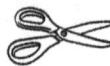

When cutting out the boxes on the left, do not cut this area. The letters for the next word are printed on the other side of this page.

find

Name

Write-It

find

Color-It

find

Find-It

| find | first | for | find |
| from | in | find | down |

Build-It

When cutting out the boxes on the left, do not cut this area. The letters for the next word are printed on the other side of this page.

| d | f | n | i |

96

Learning High-Frequency Words © Laprea Education

use

Name

Write-It

use

Color-It

use

Find-It

| was | use | up | what |
| use | very | use | she |

Build-It

s e u

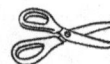

When cutting out the boxes on the left, do not cut this area. The letters for the next word are printed on the other side of this page.

may

Name

Write-It

may

Color-It

may

Find-It

| may | may | made | many |
| more | most | much | may |

Build-It

a   y   m

When cutting out the boxes on the left, do not cut this area. The letters for the next word are printed on the other side of this page.

water

Name

Write-It

water

Color-It

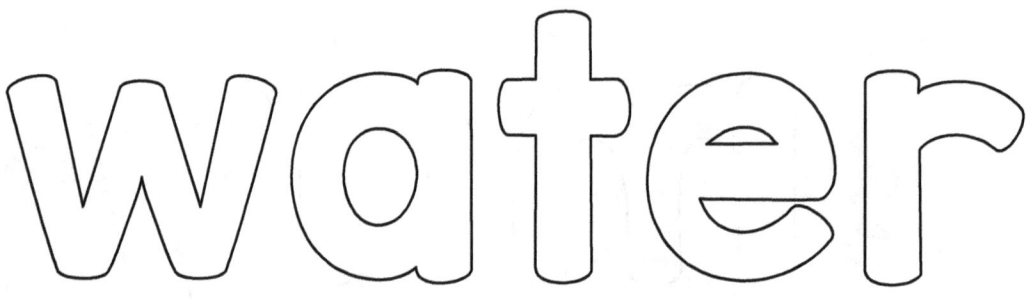

Find-It

| water | water | would | words |
| her | which | when | water |

Build-It

---

r a t w e

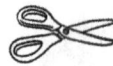

When cutting out the boxes on the left, do not cut this area. The letters for the next word are printed on the other side of this page.

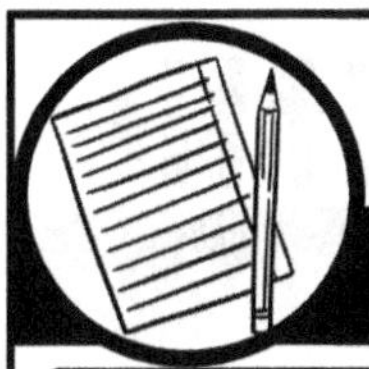

long

Name

Write-It

long

Color-It

long

Find-It

| long | like | little | only |
| long | called | long | all |

Build-It

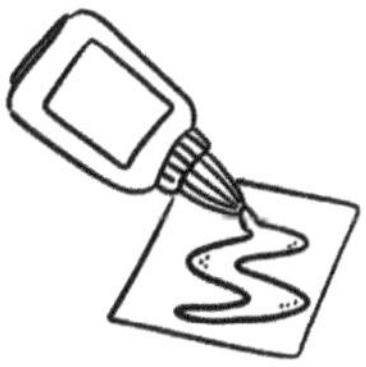

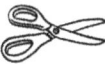

When cutting out the boxes on the left, do not cut this area. The letters for the next word are printed on the other side of this page.

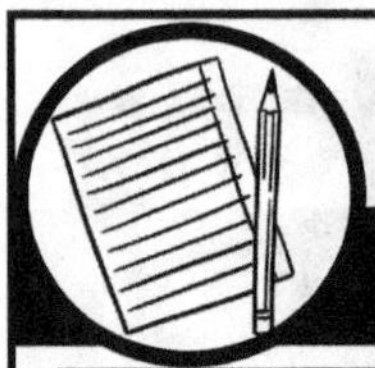

little

Name

Write-It: little

Color-It: little

Find-It:

| little | like | long | little |
| its | people | little | it |

Build-It:

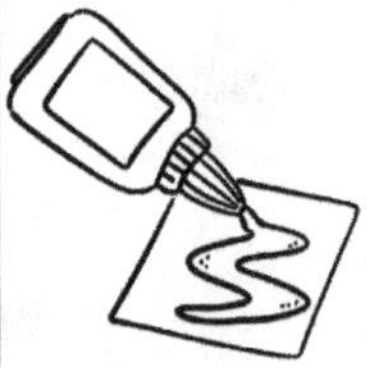

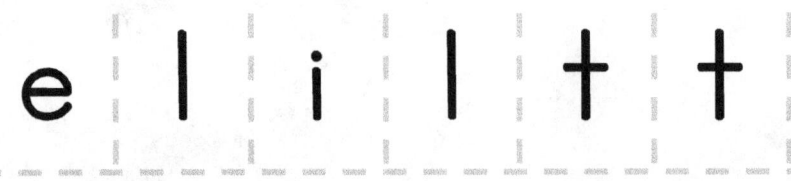

When cutting out the boxes on the left, do not cut this area. The letters for the next word are printed on the other side of this page.

very

Name

Write-It

very

Color-It

very

Find-It

| very | have | very | over |
| her | other | there | very |

Build-It

y e v r

When cutting out the boxes on the left, do not cut this area. The letters for the next word are printed on the other side of this page.

102

Learning High-Frequency Words © Laprea Education

after

Name

Write-It

after

Color-It

after

Find-It

after   and   always   for

about   above   after   after

Build-It

f a t r e

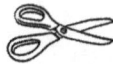

When cutting out the boxes on the left, do not cut this area. The letters for the next word are printed on the other side of this page.

103

Learning High-Frequency Words © Laprea Education

words

Name

Write-It

words

Color-It

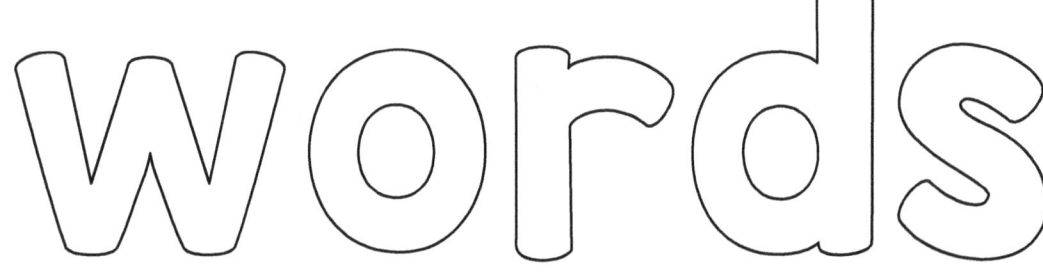

Find-It

| words | words | water | where |
| would | write | words | which |

Build-It

s r d w o

When cutting out the boxes on the left, do not cut this area. The letters for the next word are printed on the other side of this page.

called

Name

Write-It

called

Color-It

called

Find-It

| called | could | can | called |
| all | called | are | good |

Build-It

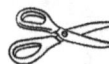

e l a c l d

When cutting out the boxes on the left, do not cut this area. The letters for the next word are printed on the other side of this page.

105

Learning High-Frequency Words © Laprea Education

just

Name

Write-It: just

Color-It: just

Find-It:

| just | its | up | use |
| first | just | most | just |

Build-It: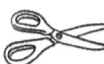

t u j s

When cutting out the boxes on the left, do not cut this area. The letters for the next word are printed on the other side of this page.

where

Name

Write-It
where

Color-It
where

Find-It
| where | words | write | where |
| with | which | water | where |

Build-It

---

e | h | w | r | e

When cutting out the boxes on the left, do not cut this area. The letters for the next word are printed on the other side of this page.

most

Name

Write-It

most

Color-It

most

Find-It

| most | many | most | more |
| most | much | first | my |

Build-It

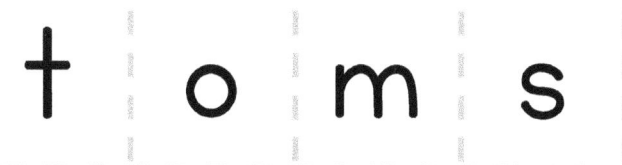

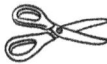

When cutting out the boxes on the left, do not cut this area. The letters for the next word are printed on the other side of this page.

108

Learning High-Frequency Words © Laprea Education

know

Name

Write-It
know

Color-It
know

Find-It

| down | know | how | know |
| now | know | no | not |

Build-It

o w k n

When cutting out the boxes on the left, do not cut this area. The letters for the next word are printed on the other side of this page.

get

Name

Write-It: get

Color-It: get

Find-It:

get	go	good	get
had	get	long	through

Build-It:

t g e

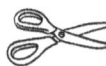

When cutting out the boxes on the left, do not cut this area. The letters for the next word are printed on the other side of this page.

110

Learning High-Frequency Words © Laprea Education

# through

Name

Write-It

through

Color-It

through

Find-It

| through | than | that | through |
| through | them | there | water |

Build-It

u g h r h o t

When cutting out the boxes on the left, do not cut this area. The letters for the next word are printed on the other side of this page.

Learning High-Frequency Words © Laprea Education

back

Name

Write-It

back

Color-It

back

Find-It

| back | ball | been | back |
| be | at | back | but |

Build-It

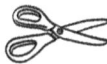

a b k c

When cutting out the boxes on the left, do not cut this area. The letters for the next word are printed on the other side of this page.

much

Name

Write-It

much

Color-It

much

Find-It

| much | most | made | much |
| my | many | most | much |

Build-It

u m h c

When cutting out the boxes on the left, do not cut this area. The letters for the next word are printed on the other side of this page.

before

Name

Write-It

before

Color-It

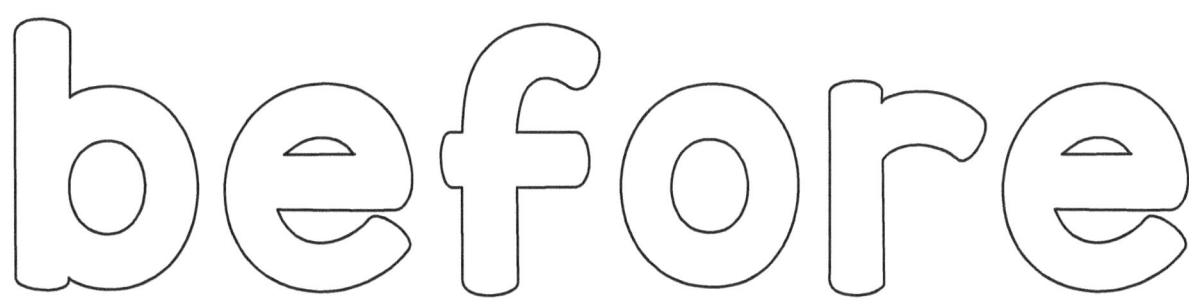

Find-It

before   after   been   before

about   be   before   water

Build-It

r e e b o f

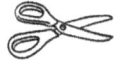

When cutting out the boxes on the left, do not cut this area. The letters for the next word are printed on the other side of this page.

go

Name

Write-It
go

Color-It
go

Find-It
| go | get | good | go |
| of | no | go | as |

Build-It
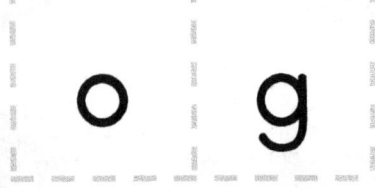

When cutting out the boxes on the left, do not cut this area. The letters for the next word are printed on the other side of this page.

Learning High-Frequency Words © Laprea Education

good

Name

Write-It

good

Color-It

good

Find-It

| good | go | get | good |
| down | do | good | back |

Build-It

| o | o | g | d |

When cutting out the boxes on the left, do not cut this area. The letters for the next word are printed on the other side of this page.

Learning High-Frequency Words © Laprea Education

new

Name

Write-It: new

Color-It: new

Find-It:

no	new	not	new
know	now	many	new

Build-It:

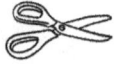

w n e

When cutting out the boxes on the left, do not cut this area. The letters for the next word are printed on the other side of this page.

write

Name

Write-It
write

Color-It
write

Find-It
where what write write
words write would were

Build-It

t w r i e

When cutting out the boxes on the left, do not cut this area. The letters for the next word are printed on the other side of this page.

www.ingramcontent.com/pod-product-compliance
Lightning Source LLC
Chambersburg PA
CBHW080346170426

43194CB00014B/2704